Missions Minded

Managing Anxiety

While Serving

Devotional

Missions Minded

Managing Anxiety

While Serving

Devotional

Dr. Lisa H. Fuller

Missions Minded Managing Anxiety While Serving Devotional

Published by Learn Realistic Habits for the Future
Southfield, MI, USA

www.LearnRealisticHabitsfortheFuture.com

Printed in the United States of America.

Interior & book cover design: Dr. Lisa H. Fuller

ISBN 13: 979-8-9997596-1-0

Unless otherwise stated, Scriptures are from the King James Version

DEDICATION

This book series is dedicated to my Ordination Board
Bishop Edgar L. Vann, II
Bishop James A. Williams, II
Bishop Daryl D. Harris

During my Ordination Board interview, I unexpectedly found myself in tears. I diligently prepared (writing my Ordination Paper, spending time in prayer, studying Scripture nightly, and reviewing Ordination Board questions). Yet in that moment, I became overwhelmed. I realized that Ordination is not a credential, but a sacred commission. Rather than disqualifying me for crying, that moment affirmed that this calling is not casual, but *holy.* God extended grace to me through the Ordination Board. I extend that same grace to others.

I am grateful.

Thank you.

To God be the glory

ACKNOWLEDGMENTS

To God be the glory for all He has done in my life!

A special thank you to Ms. Rose Pleasant
Mrs. Sally Burkes, Mrs. Marie Scott
Ms. Effoloia Frances May Young, Ms. Myrakle Young
Dr. Bola Fashola, Min. Erin Hermsen, Pastor Kay Brundidge
Mrs. Sarah Mosby, Mr. Robert Williams
Dr. Sabrina D. Black, Dr. Jan M. Newby, Min. Fran Tarver
Dr. Charlotte Joubert, Superintendent & Evan. Keeling
Bishop & Dr. Huggins, Min. Lorraine Colts
Officer Yonnell Haston, Mr. Gairyd Fuller, Ms. Zandra Mora
Mr. Cameron Fuller
&
Dr. Sherill Piscopo for support throughout the years.

May God bless you & your families with overflow, peace, and protection in Jesus name.

Amen

DISCLAIMER

Missions Minded Managing Anxiety While Serving Devotional may trigger or precipitate emotional responses. If reading this book precipitates any triggers, flashbacks, emotional responses, etc., contact and follow up with mental and/or medical health professionals. If you are a threat to yourself or others, contact 911 or 988. 988 is a 24-hour Suicide and Crisis Lifeline. (No affiliations with 911 or 988 exists.)

Stop reading *Missions Minded Managing Anxiety While Serving Devotional* if you do not accept all parts of this disclaimer.

This book does not promise any guarantees. You acknowledge you are solely responsible for your choices and the results received from this book.

Missions Minded Managing Anxiety While Serving Devotional does not provide any form of mental health or medical advice or recommendations. This book does not provide any legal or financial advice. Do not use *Missions Minded Managing Anxiety While Serving Devotional* or any section to make diagnosis for yourself or others. If you feel you are in need of mental health treatment, stop reading this book and contact a mental health or medical professional.

MAKE JESUS LORD OVER YOUR LIFE TODAY

Confess these words aloud with a sincere heart.

Lord Jesus, I repent of my sins. Jesus, I believe You died on the Cross to pay the price for my sins. Jesus, I believe You rose on the third day from the dead. Jesus, come into my heart. I transfer my trust to You this day. Jesus, I make You my personal Lord and Savior.

Prayer

Holy Spirit give Your son/ Your daughter assurance that Jesus is now their personal Lord and Savior. Thank You, Father God for giving them a new beginning. It is in Your Son, Jesus name this prayer is prayed. Amen

What The Bible Says About What You Have Just Done
Romans 10:9-10

that if thou shalt confess with thy mouth the Lord Jesus, and shalt believe in thine heart that God hath raised him from the dead, thou shalt be saved. For with the heart man believeth unto righteousness; and with the mouth confession is made unto salvation.

John 3:16-17

For God so loved the world, that he gave his only begotten Son, that whosoever believeth in him should not perish, but have everlasting life. For God sent not his Son into the world to condemn the world; but that the world through him might be saved.

MAKE JESUS LORD OVER YOUR LIFE TODAY

Praise Jesus for what you have just done!

By making Jesus your personal Lord and Savior, you now have the gift of eternal life. This means, when your physical man (body) goes back to the dirt from where it came, your spirit man (spirit) will spend eternity with Jesus.

NEXT STEPS

Now, become a member and commit to a Bible based church that teaches and preaches the unadulterated Gospel of Jesus Christ so you can grow as a disciple of Jesus. A disciple of Jesus is one who faithfully follows Jesus, learns from His teachings, and is continually transformed by the work of the Holy Spirit, resulting in a life that increasingly reflects the character, values, and mission of Jesus.

Amen

PRAYER

Dear Heavenly Father provide peace and comfort to every reader of this book series.

Behind every anxious soul, masked smile, and sad heart meet them.

According to Isaiah 61:3, give them beauty for ashes, the oil of joy for mourning, the garment of praise for the spirit of heaviness that they might be called trees of righteousness.

Holy Spirit give them assurance they are the righteous in God through Christ Jesus.
Give them assurance You are with them.
Give them assurance Your Word will not come back void, but will accomplish what You intend it to accomplish according to Isaiah 55:11.

Let them be steadfast, unmovable, always abounding in the work of the Lord according to I Corinthians 15:58.

Turn every tear of distress and discomfort into tears of joy, peace, and rest in Christ Jesus.

For in You, Jesus there is rest for their souls.

Amen.

TABLE OF CONTENTS

PREFACE

Ministry service is stressful. It is not uncommon for many serving in ministry to experience anxiety, stress, depression, emotional overwhelm, burnout, addictions, disappointment, insecurity, and doubt while serving. Those serving in ministry including spiritual leaders are human too with vulnerabilities and imperfections in need of God's grace just like everyone else. God's grace is necessary for every ministry assignment, especially ministering in an increasingly skeptical and spiritually resistant world. Being called by God does not mean immunity from struggles. Sometimes, more grace is needed given the heightened level of spiritual warfare encountered by those who serve in the ministry. It is not unusual for those serving in ministry to find themselves living out the very sermons they preach each Sunday.

Missions Minded Managing Anxiety While Serving book series emphasizes the importance of intentional and complete surrender to the Holy Spirit. Yielding to God, allows the Holy Spirit to work in and through you in ways that surpass your natural strengths, abilities, and understanding, empowering you to fulfill God's purpose with divine wisdom and supernatural power. Surrender invites an opportunity to experience God's presence, God's power, and God's direction. Allow God to work through you.

Isaiah 43:10

Ye are my witnesses, saith the LORD, and my servant whom I have chosen: that ye may know and believe me, and understand that I am he: before me there was no God formed, neither shall there be after me.

Proverbs 3:5-6

Trust in the LORD with all thine heart; And lean not unto thine own understanding. In all thy ways acknowledge him, And he shall direct thy paths.

Isaiah 55:11

so shall my word be that goeth forth out of my mouth: it shall not return unto me void, but it shall accomplish that which I please, and it shall prosper in the thing whereto I sent it.

HOW THIS DEVOTIONAL WORKS

Missions Minded Managing Anxiety While Serving is designed to be utilized both individually and in small group settings.

Prayerfully reflect and journal in *Missions Minded Managing Anxiety While Serving Devotional* while reading and working through *Missions Minded Managing Anxiety While Serving* book and workbook.

Missions Minded Managing Anxiety While Serving Devotional consists of three sections: Scripture Reflection, Personal Ministry Reflection, and Ministry Assignment Reflection.

Scripture Reflection provides an opportunity to prayerfully read, study, and reflect on Scripture. Ask Holy Spirit to reveal to you and deepen your understanding of His Word.

Personal Ministry Reflection provides an opportunity for self-awareness and deeper insight into thoughts, decisions, and responses that create and contribute to anxiety and influence emotional overwhelm while serving in ministry, (past and present).

Ministry Activity Reflection directs readers to evaluate and reflect upon specific ministry experiences and patterns across ministry service.

Note: Increase awareness of triggers and patterns that provoke anxiety can support the development of healthier responses, strengthen positive adaptive coping, and promote greater emotional and spiritual well-being when encountering similar circumstances in the future.

HOW THIS DEVOTIONAL WORKS

While completing *Missions Minded Managing Anxiety While Serving* series, **commit to:**

1. Prayerfully surrendering your heart to receive, God's peace, revelation, and impartation.

2. Prayerfully seeking God while completing the **entire** *Missions Minded Managing Anxiety While Serving* series.

3. Creating a quiet, distraction-free environment while completing the *Missions Minded Managing Anxiety While Serving* series.

4. Daily prayer.

5. Daily Scripture reading.

6. Reflection and journaling of ministry challenges in the personal ministry reflection and ministry activity reflection sections.

HOW THIS DEVOTIONAL WORKS

Transformation

Reading and completing *Missions Minded Managing Anxiety While Serving* series is only the beginning.

In *Missions Minded Managing Anxiety While Serving,* Chapter 4 discusses the Word of God. **Make God's Word your first option. It should not be your second or third option or your "go to" option after everything else fails.**

Surrendering to God means hiding His Word in your heart and allowing Holy Spirit to supernaturally shape your thoughts, direct your decisions, and transform you from the inside out.

Transformation occurs over time. Change is the result of personal experiences of God's faithfulness-one experience at a time. Think of it as your "default response" or "default reflex response." In other words, your "spiritual reflex" which results in a response with faith rather than anxiety, fear, doubt, and emotional overwhelm. Let God's Word be your first response in every season of your life including your ministry. The only way our flesh can do this is with help from the Holy Spirit.

HOW THIS DEVOTIONAL WORKS

Romans 12:2

And be not conformed to this world: but be ye transformed by the renewing of your mind, that ye may prove what is that good, and acceptable, and perfect, will of God.

Psalm 16:11

Thou wilt shew me the path of life: In thy presence is fulness of joy; At thy right hand there are pleasures for evermore.

James 1:21

Wherefore lay apart all filthiness and superfluity of naughtiness, and receive with meekness the engrafted word, which is able to save your souls.

Please Note

Do not ignore danger and warnings. However, I know from years of personal experiences with God, the Holy Spirit will warn you of danger. Spending time in God's presence through prayer deepens one's relationship with God and allows one to confidently hear and discern His voice.

Do Not Rush Through This Series.

Take your time.

SECTION I

SCRIPTURE REFLECTION

Hebrews 4:12

For the word of God is quick, and powerful, and sharper than any twoedged sword, piercing even to the dividing asunder of soul and spirit, and of the joints and marrow, and is a discerner of the thoughts and intents of the heart.

II Timothy 3:16

All scripture is given by inspiration of God, and is profitable for doctrine, for reproof, for correction, for instruction in righteousness:

The Word of God is living, transformational, and renewing. Readers of the Holy Scriptures have the privilege of hearing what God is saying. Holy Scriptures provide God's perspective rather than our own perspective.

Prayerfully read, study, and reflect on the following Scriptures. Do not limit your study to the selected Scripture passages. It is recommended that you read the entire chapter as well as the entire book for the referenced verse(s) to gain a more complete understanding of the biblical context, deepen your comprehension of God's message, and accurately interpret the intended meaning of the text. More importantly, ask Holy Spirit to give you revelation.

Send Me

Isaiah 6:1-8

In the year that king Uzziah died I saw also the Lord sitting upon a throne, high and lifted up, and his train filled the temple. Above it stood the seraphims: each one had six wings; with twain he covered his face, and with twain he covered his feet, and with twain he did fly. And one cried unto another, and said, Holy, holy, holy, is the LORD of hosts: the whole earth is full of his glory. And the posts of the door moved at the voice of him that cried, and the house was filled with smoke. Then said I, Woe is me! for I am undone; because I am a man of unclean lips, and I dwell in the midst of a people of unclean lips: for mine eyes have seen the King, the LORD of hosts. Then flew one of the seraphims unto me, having a live coal in his hand, which he had taken with the tongs from off the altar: and he laid it upon my mouth, and said, Lo, this hath touched thy lips; and thine iniquity is taken away, and thy sin purged. Also I heard the voice of the Lord, saying, Whom shall I send, and who will go for us? Then said I, Here am I; send me.

What is God saying to you through the Scripture(s)?

____

____

____

____

____

____

____

I Am Chosen To Be A Witness For Jesus

Isaiah 43:10

Ye are my witnesses, saith the LORD , and my servant whom I have chosen: that ye may know and believe me, and understand that I am he: before me there was no God formed, neither shall there be after me.

What is God saying to you through the Scripture(s)?

I Am Chosen To Be A Witness For Jesus

Matthew 28:18-20

And Jesus came and spake unto them, saying, All power is given unto me in heaven and in earth. Go ye therefore, and teach all nations, baptizing them in the name of the Father, and of the Son, and of the Holy Ghost: teaching them to observe all things whatsoever I have commanded you: and, lo, I am with you alway, even unto the end of the world. Amen.

What is God saying to you through the Scripture(s)?

I Am Chosen To Be A Witness For Jesus

Mark 3:13-15

And he goeth up into a mountain, and calleth unto him whom he would: and they came unto him. And he ordained twelve, that they should be with him, and that he might send them forth to preach, and to have power to heal sicknesses, and to cast out devils:

What is God saying to you through the Scripture(s)?

I Am Chosen To Be A Witness For Jesus

Acts 1:8

But ye shall receive power, after that the Holy Ghost is come upon you: and ye shall be witnesses unto me both in Jerusalem, and in all Judæa, and in Samaria, and unto the uttermost part of the earth.

What is God saying to you through the Scripture(s)?

I Am Serving By The Grace of God

Ephesians 3:16-20

that he would grant you, according to the riches of his glory, to be strengthened with might by his Spirit in the inner man; that Christ may dwell in your hearts by faith; that ye, being rooted and grounded in love, may be able to comprehend with all saints what is the breadth, and length, and depth, and height; and to know the love of Christ, which passeth knowledge, that ye might be filled with all the fulness of God. Now unto him that is able to do exceeding abundantly above all that we ask or think, according to the power that worketh in us,

What is God saying to you through the Scripture(s)?

I Am Serving By The Grace of God

Philippians 4:13

I can do all things through Christ which strengtheneth me.

What is God saying to you through the Scripture(s)?

I Am Serving By The Grace of God

Luke 1:37

For with God nothing shall be impossible.

What is God saying to you through the Scripture(s)?

I Have Power, Love, and A Sound Mind

II Timothy 1:7

For God hath not given us the spirit of fear; but of power, and of love, and of a sound mind.

What is God saying to you through the Scripture(s)?

I Have Power, Love, and A Sound Mind

Psalm 139:14

I will praise thee; for I am fearfully and wonderfully made: Marvellous are thy works; And that my soul knoweth right well.

What is God saying to you through the Scripture(s)?

I Have Power, Love, and A Sound Mind

Philippians 4:6-7

Be careful for nothing; but in every thing by prayer and supplication with thanksgiving let your requests be made known unto God. And the peace of God, which passeth all understanding, shall keep your hearts and minds through Christ Jesus.

What is God saying to you through the Scripture(s)?

Serving Is An Opportunity To Glory God

Romans 8:28

And we know that all things work together for good to them that love God, to them who are the called according to his purpose.

What is God saying to you through the Scripture(s)?

Selah!

SECTION II

PERSONAL MINISTRY REFLECTION

PERSONAL MINISTRY REFLECTION

During the personal ministry reflection section, prayerfully invite the Holy Spirit to examine your heart as you reflect on your emotions, thoughts, attitudes, and responses throughout your years of ministry service. Journal what the Holy Spirit reveals to you.

Be honest and open with yourself. Honesty and openness allows opportunities for processing emotions and experiences which can serve as a form of debriefing. Additionally, processing of emotions also allows opportunity for personal insights and awareness, stress management by strengthening of healthy adaptive coping skills, and spiritual formation.

Note: Journaling supports activation of the parasympathetic nervous system allowing the body to move towards a state of calmness, rest, restoration, regulation, and balance. (See Missions Minded Managing Anxiety While Serving book.)

PERSONAL MINISTRY REFLECTION

Ministry service is not limited to the five-fold ministry, (Apostles, Prophets, Evangelists, Pastors, and Teachers). God strategically places every believer in areas of influence to advance His Kingdom and bring glory to His name. Whether serving in the marketplace, (finance, healthcare, education, law enforcement, the military, or other vocations), each believer has been entrusted with divine assignments to represent Jesus. Each place of influence is a mission field where God works through His people.

1. Have you experienced anxiety, fear, uncertainty, feelings of inadequacy, and emotional overwhelm before, during, or after ministry assignments? If so, how have these feelings distracted you from hearing clearly what the Holy Spirit is saying and serving wholeheartedly?

2. Identify recurring emotional, behavioral, and spiritual patterns that influence your attitudes, decisions, and effectiveness in ministry service. Describe those patterns and consider how they have impacted and limited your ministry service.

3. What has God revealed to you about His faithfulness as you served despite feelings of anxiety, fear, uncertainty, feelings of inadequacy, and emotional overwhelm?

PERSONAL MINISTRY REFLECTION

PERSONAL MINISTRY REFLECTION

Ministry service is not limited to the five-fold ministry, (Apostles, Prophets, Evangelists, Pastors, and Teachers). God strategically places every believer in areas of influence to advance His Kingdom and bring glory to His name. Whether serving in the marketplace, (finance, healthcare, education, law enforcement, the military, or other vocations), each believer has been entrusted with divine assignments to represent Jesus. Each place of influence is a mission field where God works through His people.

1. Have you experienced anxiety, fear, uncertainty, feelings of inadequacy, and emotional overwhelm before, during, or after ministry assignments? If so, how have these feelings distracted you from hearing clearly what the Holy Spirit is saying and serving wholeheartedly?

2. Identify recurring emotional, behavioral, and spiritual patterns that influence your attitudes, decisions, and effectiveness in ministry service. Describe those patterns and consider how they have impacted and limited your ministry service.

3. What has God revealed to you about His faithfulness as you served despite feelings of anxiety, fear, uncertainty, feelings of inadequacy, and emotional overwhelm?

PERSONAL MINISTRY REFLECTION

PERSONAL MINISTRY REFLECTION

Ministry service is not limited to the five-fold ministry, (Apostles, Prophets, Evangelists, Pastors, and Teachers). God strategically places every believer in areas of influence to advance His Kingdom and bring glory to His name. Whether serving in the marketplace, (finance, healthcare, education, law enforcement, the military, or other vocations), each believer has been entrusted with divine assignments to represent Jesus. Each place of influence is a mission field where God works through His people.

1. Have you experienced anxiety, fear, uncertainty, feelings of inadequacy, and emotional overwhelm before, during, or after ministry assignments? If so, how have these feelings distracted you from hearing clearly what the Holy Spirit is saying and serving wholeheartedly?

2. Identify recurring emotional, behavioral, and spiritual patterns that influence your attitudes, decisions, and effectiveness in ministry service. Describe those patterns and consider how they have impacted and limited your ministry service.

3. What has God revealed to you about His faithfulness as you served despite feelings of anxiety, fear, uncertainty, feelings of inadequacy, and emotional overwhelm?

PERSONAL MINISTRY REFLECTION

PERSONAL MINISTRY REFLECTION

Ministry service is not limited to the five-fold ministry, (Apostles, Prophets, Evangelists, Pastors, and Teachers). God strategically places every believer in areas of influence to advance His Kingdom and bring glory to His name. Whether serving in the marketplace, (finance, healthcare, education, law enforcement, the military, or other vocations), each believer has been entrusted with divine assignments to represent Jesus. Each place of influence is a mission field where God works through His people.

1. Have you experienced anxiety, fear, uncertainty, feelings of inadequacy, and emotional overwhelm before, during, or after ministry assignments? If so, how have these feelings distracted you from hearing clearly what the Holy Spirit is saying and serving wholeheartedly?

2. Identify recurring emotional, behavioral, and spiritual patterns that influence your attitudes, decisions, and effectiveness in ministry service. Describe those patterns and consider how they have impacted and limited your ministry service.

3. What has God revealed to you about His faithfulness as you served despite feelings of anxiety, fear, uncertainty, feelings of inadequacy, and emotional overwhelm?

PERSONAL MINISTRY REFLECTION

PERSONAL MINISTRY REFLECTION

Ministry service is not limited to the five-fold ministry, (Apostles, Prophets, Evangelists, Pastors, and Teachers). God strategically places every believer in areas of influence to advance His Kingdom and bring glory to His name. Whether serving in the marketplace, (finance, healthcare, education, law enforcement, the military, or other vocations), each believer has been entrusted with divine assignments to represent Jesus. Each place of influence is a mission field where God works through His people.

1. Have you experienced anxiety, fear, uncertainty, feelings of inadequacy, and emotional overwhelm before, during, or after ministry assignments? If so, how have these feelings distracted you from hearing clearly what the Holy Spirit is saying and serving wholeheartedly?

2. Identify recurring emotional, behavioral, and spiritual patterns that influence your attitudes, decisions, and effectiveness in ministry service. Describe those patterns and consider how they have impacted and limited your ministry service.

3. What has God revealed to you about His faithfulness as you served despite feelings of anxiety, fear, uncertainty, feelings of inadequacy, and emotional overwhelm?

PERSONAL MINISTRY REFLECTION

PERSONAL MINISTRY REFLECTION

Ministry service is not limited to the five-fold ministry, (Apostles, Prophets, Evangelists, Pastors, and Teachers). God strategically places every believer in areas of influence to advance His Kingdom and bring glory to His name. Whether serving in the marketplace, (finance, healthcare, education, law enforcement, the military, or other vocations), each believer has been entrusted with divine assignments to represent Jesus. Each place of influence is a mission field where God works through His people.

1. Have you experienced anxiety, fear, uncertainty, feelings of inadequacy, and emotional overwhelm before, during, or after ministry assignments? If so, how have these feelings distracted you from hearing clearly what the Holy Spirit is saying and serving wholeheartedly?

2. Identify recurring emotional, behavioral, and spiritual patterns that influence your attitudes, decisions, and effectiveness in ministry service. Describe those patterns and consider how they have impacted and limited your ministry service.

3. What has God revealed to you about His faithfulness as you served despite feelings of anxiety, fear, uncertainty, feelings of inadequacy, and emotional overwhelm?

PERSONAL MINISTRY REFLECTION

PERSONAL MINISTRY REFLECTION

Ministry service is not limited to the five-fold ministry, (Apostles, Prophets, Evangelists, Pastors, and Teachers). God strategically places every believer in areas of influence to advance His Kingdom and bring glory to His name. Whether serving in the marketplace, (finance, healthcare, education, law enforcement, the military, or other vocations), each believer has been entrusted with divine assignments to represent Jesus. Each place of influence is a mission field where God works through His people.

1. Have you experienced anxiety, fear, uncertainty, feelings of inadequacy, and emotional overwhelm before, during, or after ministry assignments? If so, how have these feelings distracted you from hearing clearly what the Holy Spirit is saying and serving wholeheartedly?

2. Identify recurring emotional, behavioral, and spiritual patterns that influence your attitudes, decisions, and effectiveness in ministry service. Describe those patterns and consider how they have impacted and limited your ministry service.

3. What has God revealed to you about His faithfulness as you served despite feelings of anxiety, fear, uncertainty, feelings of inadequacy, and emotional overwhelm?

PERSONAL MINISTRY REFLECTION

PERSONAL MINISTRY REFLECTION

Ministry service is not limited to the five-fold ministry, (Apostles, Prophets, Evangelists, Pastors, and Teachers). God strategically places every believer in areas of influence to advance His Kingdom and bring glory to His name. Whether serving in the marketplace, (finance, healthcare, education, law enforcement, the military, or other vocations), each believer has been entrusted with divine assignments to represent Jesus. Each place of influence is a mission field where God works through His people.

1. Have you experienced anxiety, fear, uncertainty, feelings of inadequacy, and emotional overwhelm before, during, or after ministry assignments? If so, how have these feelings distracted you from hearing clearly what the Holy Spirit is saying and serving wholeheartedly?

2. Identify recurring emotional, behavioral, and spiritual patterns that influence your attitudes, decisions, and effectiveness in ministry service. Describe those patterns and consider how they have impacted and limited your ministry service.

3. What has God revealed to you about His faithfulness as you served despite feelings of anxiety, fear, uncertainty, feelings of inadequacy, and emotional overwhelm?

PERSONAL MINISTRY REFLECTION

PERSONAL MINISTRY REFLECTION

Ministry service is not limited to the five-fold ministry, (Apostles, Prophets, Evangelists, Pastors, and Teachers). God strategically places every believer in areas of influence to advance His Kingdom and bring glory to His name. Whether serving in the marketplace, (finance, healthcare, education, law enforcement, the military, or other vocations), each believer has been entrusted with divine assignments to represent Jesus. Each place of influence is a mission field where God works through His people.

1. Have you experienced anxiety, fear, uncertainty, feelings of inadequacy, and emotional overwhelm before, during, or after ministry assignments? If so, how have these feelings distracted you from hearing clearly what the Holy Spirit is saying and serving wholeheartedly?

2. Identify recurring emotional, behavioral, and spiritual patterns that influence your attitudes, decisions, and effectiveness in ministry service. Describe those patterns and consider how they have impacted and limited your ministry service.

3. What has God revealed to you about His faithfulness as you served despite feelings of anxiety, fear, uncertainty, feelings of inadequacy, and emotional overwhelm?

PERSONAL MINISTRY REFLECTION

PERSONAL MINISTRY REFLECTION

Ministry service is not limited to the five-fold ministry, (Apostles, Prophets, Evangelists, Pastors, and Teachers). God strategically places every believer in areas of influence to advance His Kingdom and bring glory to His name. Whether serving in the marketplace, (finance, healthcare, education, law enforcement, the military, or other vocations), each believer has been entrusted with divine assignments to represent Jesus. Each place of influence is a mission field where God works through His people.

1. Have you experienced anxiety, fear, uncertainty, feelings of inadequacy, and emotional overwhelm before, during, or after ministry assignments? If so, how have these feelings distracted you from hearing clearly what the Holy Spirit is saying and serving wholeheartedly?

2. Identify recurring emotional, behavioral, and spiritual patterns that influence your attitudes, decisions, and effectiveness in ministry service. Describe those patterns and consider how they have impacted and limited your ministry service.

3. What has God revealed to you about His faithfulness as you served despite feelings of anxiety, fear, uncertainty, feelings of inadequacy, and emotional overwhelm?

PERSONAL MINISTRY REFLECTION

PERSONAL MINISTRY REFLECTION

Ministry service is not limited to the five-fold ministry, (Apostles, Prophets, Evangelists, Pastors, and Teachers). God strategically places every believer in areas of influence to advance His Kingdom and bring glory to His name. Whether serving in the marketplace, (finance, healthcare, education, law enforcement, the military, or other vocations), each believer has been entrusted with divine assignments to represent Jesus. Each place of influence is a mission field where God works through His people.

1. Have you experienced anxiety, fear, uncertainty, feelings of inadequacy, and emotional overwhelm before, during, or after ministry assignments? If so, how have these feelings distracted you from hearing clearly what the Holy Spirit is saying and serving wholeheartedly?

2. Identify recurring emotional, behavioral, and spiritual patterns that influence your attitudes, decisions, and effectiveness in ministry service. Describe those patterns and consider how they have impacted and limited your ministry service.

3. What has God revealed to you about His faithfulness as you served despite feelings of anxiety, fear, uncertainty, feelings of inadequacy, and emotional overwhelm?

PERSONAL MINISTRY REFLECTION

PERSONAL MINISTRY REFLECTION

Ministry service is not limited to the five-fold ministry, (Apostles, Prophets, Evangelists, Pastors, and Teachers). God strategically places every believer in areas of influence to advance His Kingdom and bring glory to His name. Whether serving in the marketplace, (finance, healthcare, education, law enforcement, the military, or other vocations), each believer has been entrusted with divine assignments to represent Jesus. Each place of influence is a mission field where God works through His people.

1. Have you experienced anxiety, fear, uncertainty, feelings of inadequacy, and emotional overwhelm before, during, or after ministry assignments? If so, how have these feelings distracted you from hearing clearly what the Holy Spirit is saying and serving wholeheartedly?

2. Identify recurring emotional, behavioral, and spiritual patterns that influence your attitudes, decisions, and effectiveness in ministry service. Describe those patterns and consider how they have impacted and limited your ministry service.

3. What has God revealed to you about His faithfulness as you served despite feelings of anxiety, fear, uncertainty, feelings of inadequacy, and emotional overwhelm?

PERSONAL MINISTRY REFLECTION

PERSONAL MINISTRY REFLECTION

Ministry service is not limited to the five-fold ministry, (Apostles, Prophets, Evangelists, Pastors, and Teachers). God strategically places every believer in areas of influence to advance His Kingdom and bring glory to His name. Whether serving in the marketplace, (finance, healthcare, education, law enforcement, the military, or other vocations), each believer has been entrusted with divine assignments to represent Jesus. Each place of influence is a mission field where God works through His people.

1. Have you experienced anxiety, fear, uncertainty, feelings of inadequacy, and emotional overwhelm before, during, or after ministry assignments? If so, how have these feelings distracted you from hearing clearly what the Holy Spirit is saying and serving wholeheartedly?

2. Identify recurring emotional, behavioral, and spiritual patterns that influence your attitudes, decisions, and effectiveness in ministry service. Describe those patterns and consider how they have impacted and limited your ministry service.

3. What has God revealed to you about His faithfulness as you served despite feelings of anxiety, fear, uncertainty, feelings of inadequacy, and emotional overwhelm?

PERSONAL MINISTRY REFLECTION

SECTION III

MINISTRY SERVICE REFLECTION

Allow the Holy Spirit to Guide

Prayerfully ask the Holy Spirit to bring to your remembrance specific ministry assignments and experiences from the past and present, include ministry assignments and experiences that occurred over the past weeks, months, and years. Reflect upon individual and group ministry experiences, local outreach service, and mission assignments within your local community, across the nation, and internationally.

As you prayerfully journey through the *Missions Minded Managing Anxiety While Serving* series, allow Holy Spirit to reveal emotional, situational, and environmental triggers that are catalysts for anxiety, fear, doubt, and emotional overwhelm. Build on insights and awarenesses gained through the Personal Ministry Reflection section. Integrate and reflect on journal notes to develop greater awareness of recurring patterns, emotional responses, and spiritual lessons that lead to deeper understanding and dependence on God. Reflect upon how God is using these experiences to shape and mold you *on the Potter's wheel* and develop your ministry effectiveness. Invite the Holy Spirit to supernaturally transform you so future ministry service may be approached with greater faith, spiritual maturity, emotional resilience, and total dependence on God.

MINISTRY ACTIVITY

1. Anxiety Triggering Activity (present or past):

List one activity at a time.

____

____

____

____

2. Emotional Factors Triggering Anxiety and Emotional Overwhelm.

____

____

____

____

3. Situational Factors Triggering Anxiety and Emotional Overwhelm.

____

____

____

____

4. Environmental Factors Triggering Anxiety and Emotional Overwhelm.

____

____

____

____

5. Describe the emotional transformation you experienced once surrendering to God.

____

____

____

____

____

6. How did total surrender to God affect your capacity to minister with confidence and effectiveness?

____

____

____

____

____

7. List strategies, practical ministry tools, and biblical resources you utilized to manage anxiety and emotional overwhelm, (both naturally and spiritually) deepening your dependence on God and cultivating greater confidence in the leading and empowerment of the Holy Spirit?

____

____

____

____

____

MINISTRY ACTIVITY

1. Anxiety Triggering Activity (present or past):

List one activity at a time.

____

____

____

____

2. Emotional Factors Triggering Anxiety and Emotional Overwhelm.

____

____

____

____

3. Situational Factors Triggering Anxiety and Emotional Overwhelm.

____

____

____

____

4. Environmental Factors Triggering Anxiety and Emotional Overwhelm.

____

____

____

____

5. Describe the emotional transformation you experienced once surrendering to God.

____

____

____

____

____

6. How did total surrender to God affect your capacity to minister with confidence and effectiveness?

____

____

____

____

____

7. List strategies, practical ministry tools, and biblical resources you utilized to manage anxiety and emotional overwhelm, (both naturally and spiritually) deepening your dependence on God and cultivating greater confidence in the leading and empowerment of the Holy Spirit?

____

____

____

____

____

MINISTRY ACTIVITY

1. Anxiety Triggering Activity (present or past):

List one activity at a time.

____

____

____

____

2. Emotional Factors Triggering Anxiety and Emotional Overwhelm.

____

____

____

____

3. Situational Factors Triggering Anxiety and Emotional Overwhelm.

____

____

____

____

4. Environmental Factors Triggering Anxiety and Emotional Overwhelm.

____

____

____

____

5. Describe the emotional transformation you experienced once surrendering to God.

____

____

____

____

____

6. How did total surrender to God affect your capacity to minister with confidence and effectiveness?

____

____

____

____

____

7. List strategies, practical ministry tools, and biblical resources you utilized to manage anxiety and emotional overwhelm, (both naturally and spiritually) deepening your dependence on God and cultivating greater confidence in the leading and empowerment of the Holy Spirit?

____

____

____

____

____

MINISTRY ACTIVITY

1. Anxiety Triggering Activity (present or past):

List one activity at a time.

____

____

____

____

2. Emotional Factors Triggering Anxiety and Emotional Overwhelm.

____

____

____

____

3. Situational Factors Triggering Anxiety and Emotional Overwhelm.

____

____

____

____

4. Environmental Factors Triggering Anxiety and Emotional Overwhelm.

____

____

____

____

5. Describe the emotional transformation you experienced once surrendering to God.

____

____

____

____

____

6. How did total surrender to God affect your capacity to minister with confidence and effectiveness?

____

____

____

____

____

7. List strategies, practical ministry tools, and biblical resources you utilized to manage anxiety and emotional overwhelm, (both naturally and spiritually) deepening your dependence on God and cultivating greater confidence in the leading and empowerment of the Holy Spirit?

____

____

____

____

____

MINISTRY ACTIVITY

1. Anxiety Triggering Activity (present or past):

List one activity at a time.

____

____

____

____

2. Emotional Factors Triggering Anxiety and Emotional Overwhelm.

____

____

____

____

3. Situational Factors Triggering Anxiety and Emotional Overwhelm.

____

____

____

____

4. Environmental Factors Triggering Anxiety and Emotional Overwhelm.

____

____

____

____

5. Describe the emotional transformation you experienced once surrendering to God.

____

____

____

____

____

6. How did total surrender to God affect your capacity to minister with confidence and effectiveness?

____

____

____

____

____

7. List strategies, practical ministry tools, and biblical resources you utilized to manage anxiety and emotional overwhelm, (both naturally and spiritually) deepening your dependence on God and cultivating greater confidence in the leading and empowerment of the Holy Spirit?

____

____

____

____

____

MINISTRY ACTIVITY

1. Anxiety Triggering Activity (present or past):

List one activity at a time.

____

____

____

____

2. Emotional Factors Triggering Anxiety and Emotional Overwhelm.

____

____

____

____

3. Situational Factors Triggering Anxiety and Emotional Overwhelm.

____

____

____

____

4. Environmental Factors Triggering Anxiety and Emotional Overwhelm.

____

____

____

____

5. Describe the emotional transformation you experienced once surrendering to God.

____

____

____

____

____

6. How did total surrender to God affect your capacity to minister with confidence and effectiveness?

____

____

____

____

____

7. List strategies, practical ministry tools, and biblical resources you utilized to manage anxiety and emotional overwhelm, (both naturally and spiritually) deepening your dependence on God and cultivating greater confidence in the leading and empowerment of the Holy Spirit?

____

____

____

____

____

MINISTRY ACTIVITY

1. Anxiety Triggering Activity (present or past):

List one activity at a time.

____

____

____

____

2. Emotional Factors Triggering Anxiety and Emotional Overwhelm.

____

____

____

____

3. Situational Factors Triggering Anxiety and Emotional Overwhelm.

____

____

____

____

4. Environmental Factors Triggering Anxiety and Emotional Overwhelm.

____

____

____

____

5. Describe the emotional transformation you experienced once surrendering to God.

____

____

____

____

____

6. How did total surrender to God affect your capacity to minister with confidence and effectiveness?

____

____

____

____

____

7. List strategies, practical ministry tools, and biblical resources you utilized to manage anxiety and emotional overwhelm, (both naturally and spiritually) deepening your dependence on God and cultivating greater confidence in the leading and empowerment of the Holy Spirit?

____

____

____

____

____

MINISTRY ACTIVITY

1. Anxiety Triggering Activity (present or past):

List one activity at a time.

____

____

____

____

2. Emotional Factors Triggering Anxiety and Emotional Overwhelm.

____

____

____

____

3. Situational Factors Triggering Anxiety and Emotional Overwhelm.

____

____

____

____

4. Environmental Factors Triggering Anxiety and Emotional Overwhelm.

____

____

____

____

5. Describe the emotional transformation you experienced once surrendering to God.

____

____

____

____

____

6. How did total surrender to God affect your capacity to minister with confidence and effectiveness?

____

____

____

____

____

7. List strategies, practical ministry tools, and biblical resources you utilized to manage anxiety and emotional overwhelm, (both naturally and spiritually) deepening your dependence on God and cultivating greater confidence in the leading and empowerment of the Holy Spirit?

____

____

____

____

____

MINISTRY ACTIVITY

1. Anxiety Triggering Activity (present or past):

List one activity at a time.

____

____

____

____

2. Emotional Factors Triggering Anxiety and Emotional Overwhelm.

____

____

____

____

3. Situational Factors Triggering Anxiety and Emotional Overwhelm.

____

____

____

____

4. Environmental Factors Triggering Anxiety and Emotional Overwhelm.

____

____

____

____

5. Describe the emotional transformation you experienced once surrendering to God.

____

____

____

____

____

6. How did total surrender to God affect your capacity to minister with confidence and effectiveness?

____

____

____

____

____

7. List strategies, practical ministry tools, and biblical resources you utilized to manage anxiety and emotional overwhelm, (both naturally and spiritually) deepening your dependence on God and cultivating greater confidence in the leading and empowerment of the Holy Spirit?

____

____

____

____

____

MINISTRY ACTIVITY

1. Anxiety Triggering Activity (present or past):

List one activity at a time.

____

____

____

____

2. Emotional Factors Triggering Anxiety and Emotional Overwhelm.

____

____

____

____

3. Situational Factors Triggering Anxiety and Emotional Overwhelm.

____

____

____

____

4. Environmental Factors Triggering Anxiety and Emotional Overwhelm.

____

____

____

____

5. Describe the emotional transformation you experienced once surrendering to God.

6. How did total surrender to God affect your capacity to minister with confidence and effectiveness?

7. List strategies, practical ministry tools, and biblical resources you utilized to manage anxiety and emotional overwhelm, (both naturally and spiritually) deepening your dependence on God and cultivating greater confidence in the leading and empowerment of the Holy Spirit?

MINISTRY ACTIVITY

1. Anxiety Triggering Activity (present or past):

List one activity at a time.

____

____

____

____

2. Emotional Factors Triggering Anxiety and Emotional Overwhelm.

____

____

____

____

3. Situational Factors Triggering Anxiety and Emotional Overwhelm.

____

____

____

____

4. Environmental Factors Triggering Anxiety and Emotional Overwhelm.

____

____

____

____

5. Describe the emotional transformation you experienced once surrendering to God.

____

____

____

____

____

6. How did total surrender to God affect your capacity to minister with confidence and effectiveness?

____

____

____

____

____

7. List strategies, practical ministry tools, and biblical resources you utilized to manage anxiety and emotional overwhelm, (both naturally and spiritually) deepening your dependence on God and cultivating greater confidence in the leading and empowerment of the Holy Spirit?

____

____

____

____

____

PRAYER

Father God, I come to You

in the matchless and mighty name of Jesus.

Please provide each person reading

Missions Minded Managing Anxiety While

Serving series victory in every area of their life where

anxiety and emotional overwhelm exits.

Give them Your peace that passes all understanding.

Help them to focus on You.

Decrease their flesh and

increase the power of the Holy Spirit in them.

Lord Jesus, increase their faith to go forth and

complete Your will.

It is in Jesus name this prayer is prayed.

Amen

RESOURCES

988 is a 24-hour Suicide and Crisis Lifeline

(No affiliations with 911 or 988 exists.)

Discern Life Consultants Health

*Psychiatric Services

*Community Mental Health Fairs

(Psychiatric Services exclusively for Michigan.)

Discern Life & Career Transitions

*Life Coaching

*Professional Life Transition Coaching

-Following Divorce

-Transitioning into 2nd Career

-Transitioning into Retirement

Life Coaching for Those In Ministry

-Groups for Senior Pastors

-Groups for Clergy (Pastors, Elders, Licensed Ministers)

-Groups for Missionaries

DiscernLifeConsultants@gmail.com

God heals supernaturally, over time, and by the use of clinicians. It is **okay** to seek professional mental health services.

ABOUT THE AUTHOR

Dr. Lisa H. Fuller, Discern Life Consultants Health CEO and CMO, has practiced psychiatry for over three decades, is an international keynote speaker, author, mentor, and missionary (leading mission teams on the continents of Africa, Asia, Europe, & North America with focus on crisis and trauma, leadership development, and spirituality). Dr. Fuller has an earned medical degree, Doctor of Osteopathic Medicine (DO) as well as an earned Doctorate degree in Ministry (DMin). Dr. Fuller is an Apostle and Senior Pastor of Christ's Arms Reaching Everywhere Ministries, part of the Evangel Association of Churches and Ministries network where she has been appointed as a member of the Apostolic Bishop Board.

Recipient of:

- Outstanding Leadership in Global Missions, Second Ebenezer Church, Bishop Edgar L. Vann, II, Detroit, MI
- Distinguished Servanthood Honor, Liberian Evangelical Baptist Convention, Ganta, Liberia
- Humanitarian & Master Teacher Award, Rapid Response Chaplain Corps, Detroit, MI

Speaking, Trainings, Academic Appointments (past & present)

- Wayne State University School of Medicine Department of Psychiatry & Behavioral Neurosciences/ Emergency Psychiatry, Assistant Professor, Detroit, MI
- Bulgaria Ecumenical Theological Seminary Guest Professor, Sofia, Bulgaria
- DayStar University Department of Psychology, Crisis & Trauma Training, Guest Professor, Nairobi, Kenya
- Nairobi Women's Hospital/ Gender Violence Unit, Trauma & Burnout, Keynote Speaker, Nairobi, Kenya
- Missions and Grief & Loss Courses Instructor, Destiny School of Ministry, Roseville, MI

- Crisis & Trauma Training, Global Projects Hope, Help & Healing, Haiti, Spain, Panama, Liberia
- Mental Health in the African American Community, Keynote Speaker, U.S. Army Corps of Engineers, Detroit, MI
- Mental Health Training for Chaplains, Rapid Response Chaplain Corps, Detroit, MI

Articles featuring Dr. Lisa H. Fuller appeared in:

- The US Times
  https://theustimes.com/dr-fullershess-her-unique-career-odyssey/
- Business Shark Magazine
  https://businesssharksmagazine.com/dr-fuller-defying-the-odds-andovercoming-obstacles/

Dr. Fuller is the Founder and Overseer of Lisa H. Fuller Ministries and Founder of Learn Realistic Habits for the Future publishing company. 2017-2025, Dr. Fuller hosted, “A Word of Encouragement,” an eight-year live radio ministry broadcast serving listeners across the greater Detroit metropolitan region, the Cincinnati metropolitan area, southeastern Indiana, and northern Kentucky.

You can purchase Dr. Fuller’s books:

on

Amazon

and where books are sold.

To Contact Dr. Lisa H. Fuller Visit:

https://DrLisaHFuller.com/

https://ChristsArmsReachingEverywhere.org/

https://LearnRealisticHabitsForTheFuture.com/

https://DiscernLifeConsultants.com/

BOOKS

by

Dr. Lisa H. Fuller

MENTAL HEALTH

God's Compassion Toward Me

De-Compress Your Stress

40 Ways To Reduce Stress

MENTAL HEALTH

Mission Minded Managing
Anxiety While Serving

Mission Minded Managing
Anxiety While Serving
Workbook

Mission Minded Managing
Anxiety While Serving
Devotional

DEVOTIONAL

Women's 30 plus 1 Day
Devotional & Journal

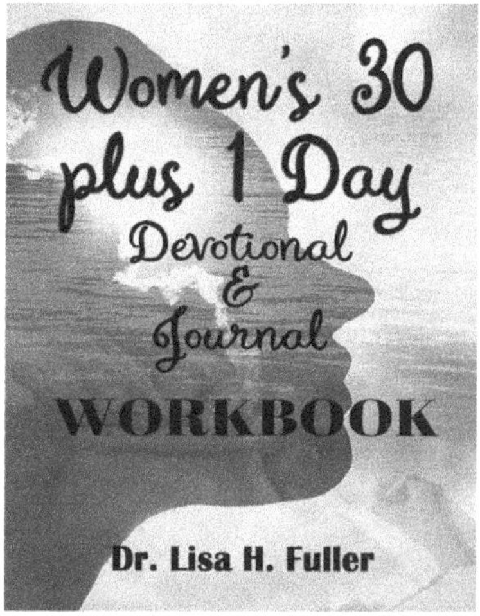

Women's 30 plus 1 Day
Devotional & Journal Workbook

You Already Have...All of the Tools That You Need

CHILDREN'S MINISTRY

God is Love
I John 4:8b

Dios Es Amor
I Juan 4:8b

www.ingramcontent.com/pod-product-compliance
Lightning Source LLC
LaVergne TN
LVHW050922210926
848482LV00012B/498